Pop & Rock Hits
INSTRUMENTAL SOLOS

CONTENTS

Arranged by Bill Galliford, Ethan Neuburg and Tod Edmondson

© 2011 Alfred Music Publishing Co., Inc.
All Rights Reserved. Printed in USA.

ISBN-10: 0-7390-8010-5
ISBN-13: 978-0-7390-8010-8

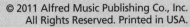

ANIMAL

Words and Music by
TIM PAGNOTTA, TYLER GLENN,
BRANDEN CAMPBELL, ELAINE DOTY
and CHRISTOPHER ALLEN

Animal - 8 - 1

8

IN MY HEAD

Words and Music by
CLAUDE KELLY, JONATHAN ROTEM
and JASON DESROULEAUX

Moderate pop rock (♩ = 112)

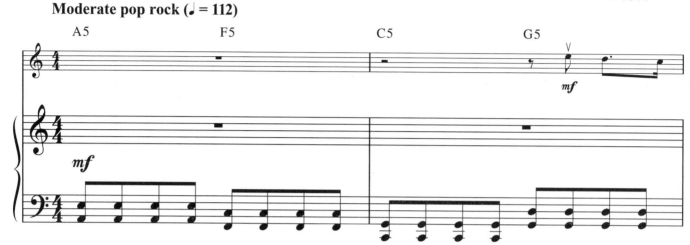

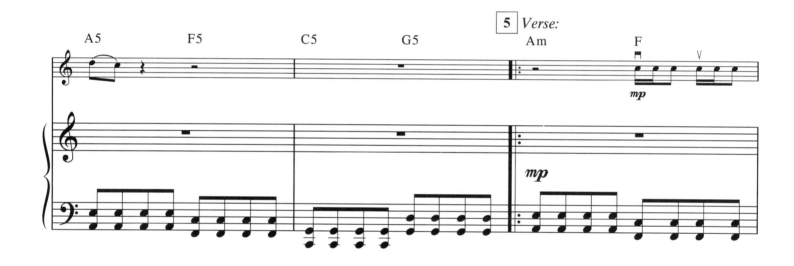

In My Head - 6 - 1

21 GUNS

Words and Music by
BILLIE JOE, GREEN DAY,
DAVID BOWIE and JOHN PHILLIPS

21 Guns - 5 - 1

21 Guns - 5 - 2

20

21 Guns - 5 - 5

FIREWORK

Words and Music by
KATY PERRY, MIKKEL ERIKSEN,
TOR ERIK HERMANSEN, SANDY WILHELM
and ESTER DEAN

Moderate rock (♩ = 126)

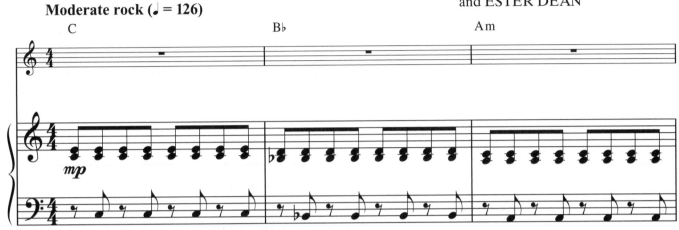

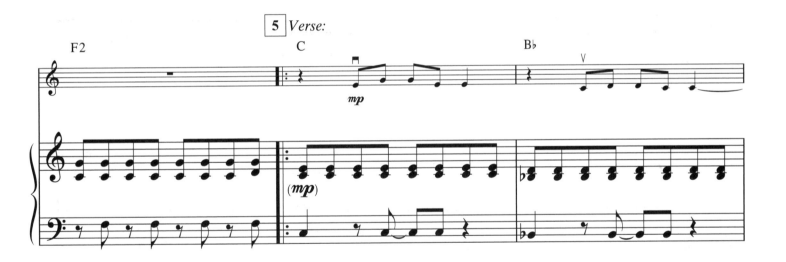

Firework - 7 - 1

Firework - 7 - 3

Firework - 7 - 5

26

BOULEVARD OF BROKEN DREAMS

Words by
BILLIE JOE

Music by
GREEN DAY

Boulevard of Broken Dreams - 4 - 4

GRENADE

Words and Music by
CLAUDE KELLY, PETER HERNANDEZ,
BRODY BROWN, PHILIP LAWRENCE,
ARI LEVINE and ANDREW WYATT

Moderately slow (♩ = 112)

Grenade - 5 - 1

Grenade - 5 - 3

JUST THE WAY YOU ARE

Words and Music by
KHALIL WALTON, PETER HERNANDEZ,
ARI LEVINE and KHARI CAIN

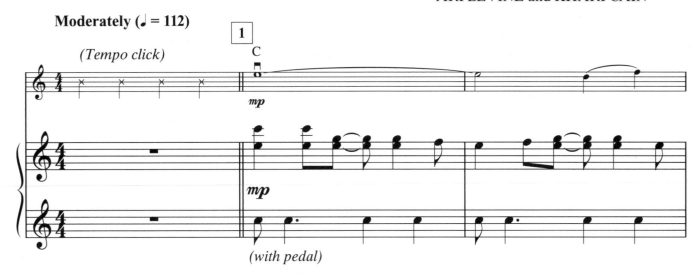

Just the Way You Are - 5 - 1

Just the Way You Are - 5 - 3

Just the Way You Are - 5 - 4

HAVEN'T MET YOU YET

Words and Music by
MICHAEL BUBLÉ, ALAN CHANG
and AMY FOSTER

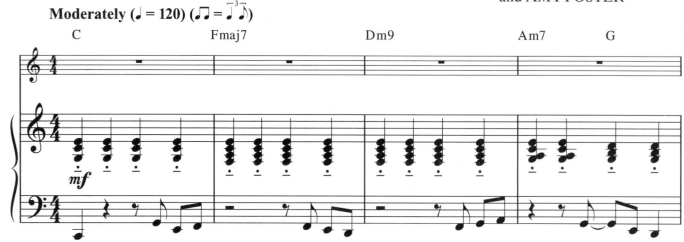

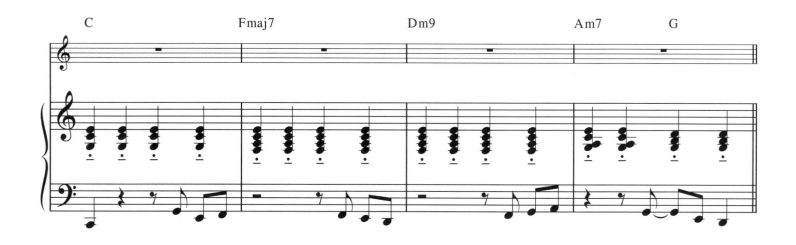

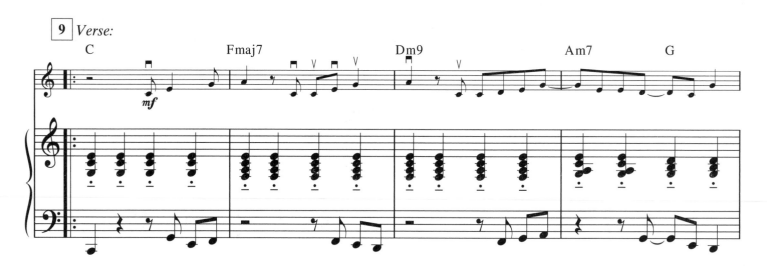

Haven't Met You Yet - 6 - 1

44

RHYTHM OF LOVE

Words and Music by
TIM LOPEZ

Rhythm of Love - 6 - 1

SMILE

Words and Music by
MATTHEW SHAFER, BLAIR DALY,
J.T. HARDING and JEREMY BOSE

Slow groove, half-time feel (♩ = 72)

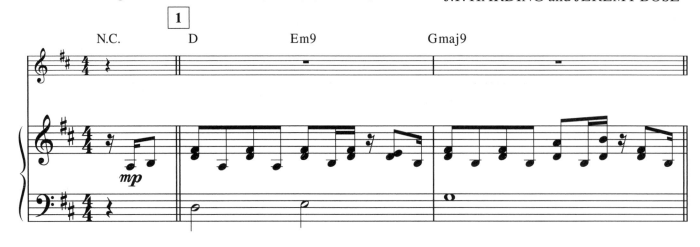

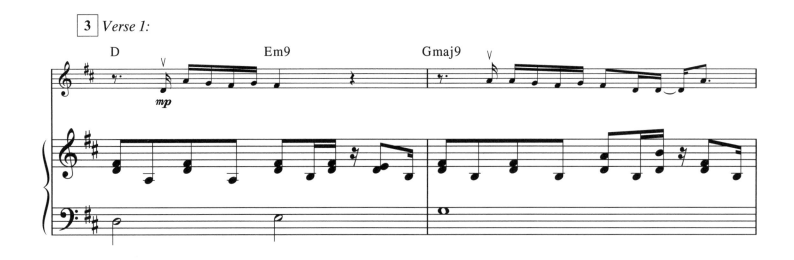

3 *Verse 1:*

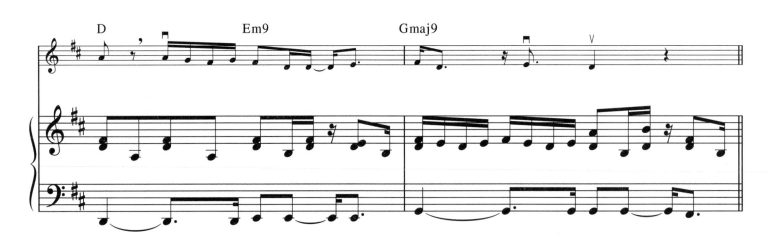

Smile - 6 - 1

7 *Verses 1 (cont.) & 2:*

13 *Chorus:*

34 *Chorus:*

NEED YOU NOW

Words and Music by
DAVE HAYWOOD, CHARLES KELLEY,
HILLARY SCOTT and JOSH KEAR

Need You Now - 5 - 1